JAN 1 8 2000

JAN 1 8 2000

ISRAEL

the culture

Debbie Smith

A Bobbie Kalman Book

The Lands, Peoples, and Cultures Series

Crabtree Publishing Company

The Lands, Peoples, and Cultures Series

Created by Bobbie Kalman

Coordinating editor
Ellen Rodger

Consulting editor
Virginia Mainprize

Project development, writing, editing, and design
First Folio Resource Group, Inc.
Pauline Beggs
Tom Dart
Marlene Elliott
Kathryn Lane
Debbie Smith

Separations and film
Dot 'n Line Image Inc.

Printer
Worzalla Publishing Company

Special thanks to
Shawky J. Fahel, J. G. Group of Companies; David H. Goldberg, Ph.D., Canada-Israel Committee; Steven Katari; Taali Lester, Israel Government Tourist Office; Alisa Siegel and Irit Waidergorn, Consulate General of Israel; Khaleel Mohammed

Photographs
Photo Researchers, cover; Steven Allan: p. 7 (top left), p. 9 (top), p. 10, p. 20 (top), p. 23 (top), p. 25 (top), p. 29 (right), p. 30 (both); David Bartruff/Corbis: p. 11 (bottom right); Joel Fishman/Photo Researchers: p. 17 (bottom); Gordon Gahan/Photo Researchers: p. 23 (bottom right); Louis Goldman/Photo Researchers: p. 23 (left); Israel Government Tourist Office: p. 28; Annie Griffiths Belt/Corbis: p. 19 (top and left); Hanan Isachar/Corbis: p. 20 (bottom); David Lees/Corbis: p. 21 (top); Yasha Mazur/Photo Researchers: p. 7 (bottom); Richard T. Nowitz: title page, p. 3–6 (all), p. 7 (right), p. 8 (both), p. 9 (bottom), p. 11 (left and top right), p. 12, p. 14–16 (all), p. 17 (top), p. 18, p. 22 (both), p. 24 (both), p. 25 (bottom), p. 29 (left); Richard T. Nowitz/Photo Researchers: p. 21 (bottom); Paul A. Souders/Corbis: p. 13; Ted Spiegel/Corbis: p. 19 (right), p. 27

Illustrations
William Kimber. The back cover, which shows an ibex, a wild goat native to Israel. An oud, a Middle Eastern instrument similar to a lute, appears at the head of each section.

Cover: The cover photo shows the celebration of a Jewish bar mitzvah at the Wailing Wall in Jerusalem.

Title page: An Arab woman and Ultra-Orthodox Jewish men talk on payphones in Jerusalem.

Published by
Crabtree Publishing Company

350 Fifth Avenue
Suite 3308
New York
N.Y. 10118

360 York Road, RR 4
Niagara-on-the-Lake
Ontario, Canada
L0S 1J0

73 Lime Walk
Headington
Oxford OX3 7AD
United Kingdom

Cataloging in Publication Data
Smith, Debbie, 1962-
    Israel: the culture/Debbie Smith.
        p. cm.-- (Lands, peoples, and cultures series)
    Summary: Surveys the practice of various religions--Judaism, Islam, Christianity, and others--in Israel and the different customs that are part of the religious holidays and festivals.
        ISBN 0-86505-311-1 (paper). -- ISBN 0-86505-231-X (rlb.)
        1. Israel--Civilization--Juvenile literature. 2. Israel--Religion-- Juvenile literature. [1. Israel--Religion. 2. Israel--Social life and customs.] I. Title.
DS112.S64 1999
956.94--dc21

LC 98-39914
CIP

Contents

Israel: The land of faith

Israel is home to people of many **faiths**. Jews, Muslims, Druze, Christians, and Baha'is all live in this small country. Their religion guides their beliefs, influences their way of life, and inspires their **culture**. The art, music, dance, literature, and clothing of Israel all reflect religious faith in some way.

Israel is a meeting place of the old and new, of eastern and western. People wearing jeans and T-shirts shop beside others wearing **traditional** clothing. One radio station plays folk songs, while another plays rock-and-roll. An Israeli movie is featured on one theater screen, while a North American movie is featured on the screen right next to it.

Israel is still a young country. As it grows older, the challenge for all of its people will be to develop their own identity while respecting the cultures and religions of those around them.

A Muslim woman holds out her hands in prayer.

(opposite) A Christian monk wanders through the desolate Judean Desert.

A Jewish Torah scroll is so long that children can read different sections of it without getting in each other's way.

Israel's religions

To understand the people of Israel, it is important to understand a bit about their faiths or beliefs. Over 80 percent of Israel's population is Jewish. About 15 percent is Muslim. Christians, Druze, Baha'is, and many smaller religious groups make up the rest of the population. Some of these faiths, or religions have common roots and share some of the same beliefs, such as the belief in one God. It is the differences between the religions, however, that make each truly interesting.

Judaism

Judaism is over 4000 years old. Its teachings are partly based on ten commandments that God gave the Jewish people thousands of years ago. The most important teaching is that there is only one God. The Golden Rule, "Do unto others as you would have others do unto you," comes from the ten commandments.

The ten commandments are found in the Torah, the first five books of the Bible. The Torah includes other laws of Judaism and tells about the early history of the Jewish people.

Branches of Judaism

At one time, most Jews were Orthodox. They followed all the traditional laws and customs of their religion. Over time, some Jews abandoned many of the old ways and began living less Orthodox lives. Today, there are different branches of Judaism, including Orthodox, Conservative, Reform, and Reconstructionist. Each group still believes that there is only one God, but they practice their religion differently. For example, Orthodox Jews keep *kosher*, which means that they follow special dietary laws. They do not eat shellfish or pork, they do not eat milk products and meat together, and they prepare their food in special ways. People who are less Orthodox are not so strict in keeping these rules.

Torah scrolls are handwritten by scribes who write on parchment paper using a feather pen and ink from an ancient recipe. It can take a year to write a Torah because every letter and every space must be just right. A proofreader must check a scribe's work carefully.

An Ethiopian Jew prays at the Western Wall. Around him slips of paper have been tucked into the crevices of the wall. On each of these papers is someone's prayer.

A young woman chants prayers from her siddur, the Jewish prayer book.

As is the custom among ultra-Orthodox Jews, this three-year-old boy has waited until the holiday of Lag Ba'Omer to have his hair cut for the first time.

A Muslim family painted the doorway of their home to let neighbors know that they completed the **hajj**, *the pilgrimage to Mecca.*

Muslims use special movements as they pray, including bowing and pressing their heads to their prayer mats.

Islam

Islam is a religion that teaches peace, mercy, and forgiveness. People who practice Islam are called Muslims. They follow the teachings of the **prophet** Muhammad, who was born in 570 A.D., in the city of Mecca, Saudi Arabia. According to Islamic belief, Muhammad received the teachings of God, whom Muslims call Allah, through the angel Jibril, or Gabriel. As Muhammad taught Allah's messages to others, Islam spread throughout the world. Today, there are two main sects of Islam: Sunni and Shiite. Most Muslims in Israel are Sunni.

The Five Pillars of Islam

Allah's instructions are recorded in the Qur'an, a holy book that is read by Muslims all over the world. There are five main principles, called the Five Pillars of Islam. The first pillar is that Muslims must declare that there is no God but Allah and Muhammad is his prophet. They must pray five times a day facing the Ka'bah, the most important shrine in Mecca. They are required to give charity to those in need and to fast in the daylight hours during the holy month of Ramadan. The fifth pillar of Islam is to perform the *hajj*, a **pilgrimage** to Mecca.

(left) Many different groups of Christians live in Israel. They share some of the same beliefs, but each group has its own customs and churches.

*(below, left) These Druze elders wear white turbans called **uqqals** that show that they are among the chosen few who know the secrets of their religion.*

Christianity

Christianity began in Israel almost 2000 years ago. It is based on the teachings of Jesus Christ. Jesus, a Jew born in the town of Bethlehem, in Israel, was believed to be God's son on earth. He taught people to be good and righteous. Many people, however, did not agree with Jesus' teachings, and he was **crucified**.

Jesus' life and lessons are recorded in a holy book called the New Testament. The Christian Bible also contains the Old Testament, which tells of the time before Christ.

Baha'i

The Baha'i faith is based on the teachings of Baha'u'llah. Baha'u'llah was born in Tehran, Iran, in 1817, and died in Akko, Israel, in 1892. Baha'u'llah's followers believe that he was a prophet sent by God, just like Jesus and Muhammad. Baha'u'llah taught that all religions honor the same God, and that people of all ages, races, and sexes are equal. He also taught that God wants one world society where everyone accepts and respects each other.

Druze

The Druze religion is over 800 years old and has its roots in Islam. The Druze believe that Allah's teachings were revealed to a special group, including a messenger who came after the prophet Muhammad.

Little is known about the everyday religious practices of the Druze. Even in their own community, only a small group of people who have passed difficult tests know the secrets of their religion.

 # Houses of worship

In Israel, people of all religions pray in their own buildings. Jews pray in synagogues or temples, Muslims pray in mosques, and Christians pray in churches.

Mosques

Religious Muslims pray five times a day: before sunrise, in early afternoon, in late afternoon, after sunset, and before going to bed. Many Muslims pray in a mosque, which must be quiet and clean. Worshippers leave their shoes in a courtyard so they do not dirty their holy place. They also wash their hands, feet, and face before entering the mosque to pray.

Traditional mosques have a tower, called a *ma'dhana* or minaret, from which a *muezzin*, or prayer caller, summons Muslims to prayer. A large dome covers the main prayer hall so that prayers can echo throughout the room. There is no furniture in this room. Instead, people pray on beautifully patterned rugs. A small alcove called a *mihrab*, shows the direction of the Ka'bah. If the mosque is large enough, there is also a *minbar*, or platform, on which the leader of the service, the *imam*, stands.

(above) The **mihrab** *is at the far end of the cavernous El Aqsa mosque in Jerusalem.*

Synagogues

Religious Jews pray three times a day: in the morning, afternoon, and evening. They usually pray at a synagogue, which is a place of worship, study, and celebration. Whether large or small, all synagogues have some features in common. The main room is an auditorium where people pray facing the holy Western Wall in Jerusalem. An *Aron Hakodesh*, or Holy Ark, holds the Torah scrolls. The *Ner Tamid*, or Everlasting Light, burns above the Ark. This light is a reminder that the light of the Torah will never die.

(above) The gold dome of the Shrine of the Bab, a Baha'i spiritual center in Haifa, rises above beautiful gardens.

Torah scrolls stand behind the embroidered curtain of the **Aron Hakodesh.**

(right) An Armenian priest prays at the altar in the Church of the Nativity, in Bethlehem. This is the oldest Christian church in the world and is believed to be built on the site where Jesus was born.

A time to celebrate

Hardly a month goes by in Israel when there is not some kind of holiday or festival. You might find it confusing to keep track of the dates of the celebrations, since Jewish, Muslim, and Christian holidays all follow different calendars.

Following the sun

The solar year is 365 days long or 366 days in a leap year. This is the time it takes for the earth to orbit around the sun. Christian holidays follow the solar calendar, where each new year begins on January 1 and ends on December 31.

Following the moon

The Muslim calendar is based on the lunar year. In the lunar calendar each of the twelve months begins when a new moon appears. The lunar year is approximately eleven days shorter than the solar year. A Muslim holiday that falls in the winter one year may fall in the summer six or seven years later!

The lunar year, plus one month

The Jewish calendar is also based on the lunar year, but it adds an extra month seven out of every nineteen years. This way, holidays fall at about the same time every year.

Counting the years

The Christian calendar divides time into two periods: before Jesus Christ was born (B.C.) and after he was born (A.D.). The Christian calendar will enter its 21st century in the year 2000. The Muslim calendar begins in the year 622 A.D., the year Muhammad moved from Mecca to Medina to spread Allah's message. The Muslim calendar is now in its 15th century. The Jewish calendar is the oldest of the three calendars. It begins when Adam, who according to the Bible was the first human, was created by God. The Jewish calendar is now in its 58th century.

Over the next two weeks, the full moon will wane. When it disappears completely, a new month will begin.

Jewish holidays and celebrations

Jewish holidays celebrate the harvest, honor the heroics of legendary figures, and remember national and religious anniversaries. Here are some of the Jewish holidays.

Rosh Hashanah

Rosh Hashanah is the Jewish New Year. It falls in September or October. Rosh Hashanah is the first of ten days when people think about the mistakes they made over the past year and ask for forgiveness. During the holiday, they eat apples dipped in honey to symbolize their hope that the new year will be sweet. They also send New Year's cards to one another, wishing a happy, healthy, and sweet year.

Blowing the shofar

During Rosh Hashanah, Jews remember the story of Abraham and his son Isaac. According to the Torah, Abraham, the first Jew, was told to **sacrifice** Isaac to prove his faith in God. When God realized that Abraham was ready to obey his command, he stopped Abraham and told him to sacrifice a ram instead. The *shofar* or ram's horn is blown on Rosh Hashanah to remind the Jewish people of Abraham's faith.

Yom Kippur

Yom Kippur, the Day of **Atonement**, falls ten days after Rosh Hashanah. On this holiest day of the year, people fast for 25 hours. By not drinking or eating anything, they ask forgiveness for the sins they committed in the past year. They also pray that God will inscribe their names for a good and healthy year in the "Book of Life."

It takes a lot of practice to learn how to blow a shofar!

Sukkot crowd the balconies of this apartment building.

Sukkot

Sukkot is a fall harvest festival. During this holiday, many families build *sukkot*, or huts, in their backyards. The sides are usually made of wood panels. The roof is made of long branches, with spaces left between them so that you can still see the sky. Fruits and vegetables hang on the walls and from the ceiling.

During Sukkot, many families eat in their *sukkah*. Some even sleep there. The *sukkah* is a reminder of the huts that farmers used to live in at **harvest** time to be near their crops. It is also a reminder of the temporary shelters in which the Jewish people lived as they journeyed through the desert thousands of years ago.

*(right) The **lulav** and **etrog** are symbols of the harvest that are used in ceremonies during Sukkot. The **lulav** is made up of branches from the palm, willow, and myrtle trees. The **etrog**, which looks like a lemon, comes from a tree called the citron.*

Chanukah

Chanukah (pronounced ha-ne-ka) is a festival of lights that takes place in November or December. Over 2000 years ago, the Syrian Greeks ruled Israel and would not let the Jews practice their religion. The Jews rebelled and recaptured their holy temple, which the Greeks had ruined. When the Jews went to relight the ever-burning *menorah*, they found just enough oil for one day. Then a miracle happened: the oil lasted for eight days until more oil could be brought to the temple. This is why Chanukah is celebrated for eight days.

Lighting a **menorah** *is part of the Chanukah tradition. Each night an additional candle is lit, until eight candles burn brightly.*
During Chanukah celebrations, children play a game of chance with a spinning top called a **sevivon** *or* **dreidl**.

Levivot

During Chanukah, Jewish people all over the world eat foods cooked in oil, such as *soofganiyot*, which are doughnuts, and *levivot* or *latkes*, which are potato pancakes. *Levivot* are very easy to make! Here are the ingredients you will need.

6 potatoes, grated and drained
3 eggs, lightly mixed
1 medium onion, chopped
1 tsp salt
¼ tsp pepper
¼ cup flour
2 tsp oil
2 tsp baking powder

Mix all the ingredients together except the oil. Heat the oil in the frying pan. Form flat pancake shapes with the batter. Place the *levivot* in the oil. Turn only once. Serve hot with sour cream or applesauce.

(right) At Pesach, families get rid of all their bread by burning it in the streets.

Which characters of the Purim story are these girls dressed as?

Purim

On Purim, families go to the synagogue to hear *Megillat Esther*, the Story of Esther. This story tells how the Jewish Queen Esther and her uncle Mordechai saved the Jews of Babylon by outsmarting Haman, the king's wicked advisor who wanted to kill the Jews. During Purim, every time people hear Haman's name, they make noise with noisemakers called *ra'ashanim* or *greggors*. They also eat special pastries called *hamantashen* or *oznei Haman*, which means Haman's ears. These triangular-shaped pastries are filled with jam, nuts, poppy seeds, or prunes.

ra'ashanim

oznei Haman

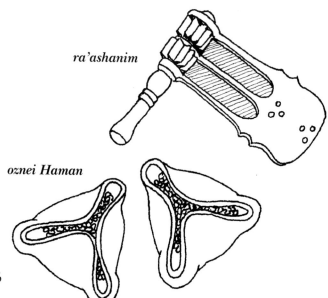

Pesach

Pesach, or Passover, celebrates the Jews' escape from slavery in Egypt thousands of years ago. The holiday lasts for seven days in Israel and for eight days outside of Israel. Before Pesach, families clean their homes to get rid of every bit of leavened bread, which is bread that has yeast. In fact, in many parts of Israel it is almost impossible to find bread in stores during Pesach! For the entire holiday people eat *matzah* instead. This unleavened bread is a reminder that the Jews left Egypt in such a hurry that they did not even have time to let their bread rise.

On Pesach, families gather for a special meal called a *seder*. During the *seder*, they read the *hagaddah*, which tells the story of Pesach, and they eat special foods. Just before the meal is served, a piece of *matzah* is broken in half. This unleavened bread is called the *afikoman*. The leader of the *seder* hides one half of the *afikoman*. At the end of the meal, children search for it in every corner of the home. The child who finds the *afikoman* gets a present.

The Pesech seder

Each of these items plays a special part during this symbolic meal.

❶ This flat, unleavened bread is *matzah*.

❷ Drinking four glasses of wine, or grape juice for younger children, is part of the *seder* tradition.

❸ Families gather around the table to read the story of Pesach from the *hagaddah*.

❹ People dip *karpas*, or greens, in salt water to remind them of the Jews' tears when they were slaves.

❺ A roasted egg reminds people of the destruction of the holy temple. Its shape is also a symbol of the continuity of life.

❻ People eat *marror*, or bitter herbs, as a reminder of the bitter lives that the Jews lived as slaves.

❼ The shankbone is a reminder of God's outstretched arm, which led the Jews out of Egypt.

❽ *Karpas,* or greens are a sign of spring, when Pesach is celebrated.

❾ *Charoset* is a mixture of apples, nuts, and wine or grape juice. It is a reminder of the mortar that the Jews used to build bricks in Egypt.

Muslim holidays remember stories that are described in the Islamic holy book, the Qur'an. They also mark events that took place during the life of the prophet Muhammad. The most important holidays are Id ul-Fitr and Id ul-Adha.

Ramadan

Ramadan is the ninth month of the Muslim calendar. It is considered a holy month because Muhammad first received Allah's messages during Ramadan. Adults and many older children spend Ramadan praying, and fasting from sunrise to sunset. Fasting teaches them to value the good things that Allah has provided them and to remember the poor and the hungry. It also teaches **self-discipline.**

Id ul-Fitr

As soon as the new moon appears, Ramadan ends, and the great celebration of Id ul-Fitr, the Festival of Fast-Breaking, begins. People prepare for the holiday by giving to charity, called Zakat ul-Fitr. The money is used to buy food for the holiday for Muslims who cannot afford it. People celebrate Id ul-Fitr by praying at home and at the mosque. They visit relatives for a special meal in the middle of the day, often bringing cakes, dried fruits, and other gifts. In the middle of the night, children knock on doors in the neighborhood, beating on the *tabla*, a Middle-Eastern drum, and singing "You who are asleep wake up and pray to Allah." In exchange, children are given sweets or money.

During Ramadan, thousands of Muslims journey to Jerusalem to pray at their holy site, the Dome of the Rock.

Id ul-Adha

Because Judaism and Islam have common roots, some holidays celebrate similar events. Id ul-Adha is the Festival of Sacrifice. This holiday recalls almost the same story as Rosh Hashanah, except in this version, Abraham was asked to sacrifice his son Ishmael, not Isaac. When Abraham proved that he was prepared to obey Allah's command, he was told to sacrifice a lamb instead. On this holiday, Muslims go to the mosque in their finest clothes to pray. To remember Abraham's sacrifice, they kill a sheep, goat, or camel and share the meat with friends, relatives, and the poor.

(top) A family prepares sweets to take to a relative's house for Id ul-Fitr.

(above) After a day of fasting, a family sits down to a large, satisfying meal.

(right) Men pour out of a mosque during the holiday of Id ul-Fitr.

Christian holidays

The two most important Christian holidays are Christmas and Easter. They both mark important events in the life of Jesus Christ.

Christmas

Christmas marks the day that Jesus Christ was born. It is a feast day when families and friends get together, eat, and often exchange gifts. In Israel, pilgrims from all over the world gather around Manger Square in Bethlehem to attend mass, and listen to music from the Church of the Nativity. They also visit cities, such as Nazareth and Jerusalem, where Jesus spent part of his life. Like in other countries where Christmas is celebrated, families decorate their homes with Christmas trees. Children wait for the arrival of "Baba Noel," which is what Santa Claus is called in Israel.

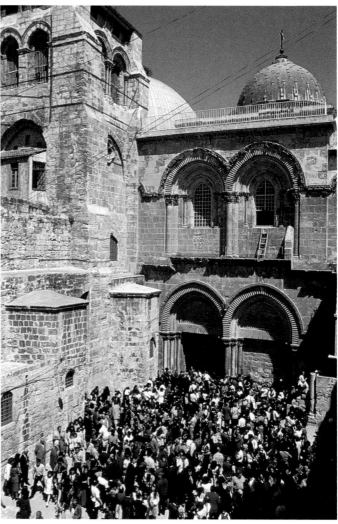

(right) During Easter, Christians crowd the courtyard outside the Church of the Holy Sepulcher in Jerusalem.

(below) Children march in a Christmas parade.

Easter

Easter is the most important feast in the Christian calendar. During this time, Christians remember Jesus' death and resurrection. The holiday begins on Holy Thursday, when Jesus had his last supper with his closest followers, and continues until Easter Sunday, when Christians believe that Jesus rose from the dead. Christians believe that Jesus died for the forgiveness of their sins and that his resurrection means they will be reborn in heaven.

During Easter, church bells ring, and services are held throughout the country. In some communities, special candles, known as Holy Lights, are lit outside churches after midnight mass and are passed from person to person.

One day that Jews, Muslims, and Christians all celebrate is a day devoted to God, or Allah. For Muslims this day is Friday, for Jews it is Saturday, and for Christians it is Sunday.

Shabbat

Shabbat, or the Jewish Sabbath, begins a little before sunset on Friday night and ends after dark on Saturday night. Families prepare for *Shabbat* as if they were welcoming a queen, the *Shabbat* queen. They dress in their finest clothes and cook a delicious meal. Before they eat their meal, they light *Shabbat* candles, drink a glass of wine or grape juice, and eat a special loaf of bread, called *challah,* after saying blessings.

Because *Shabbat* is meant to be a day of rest, Orthodox Jews do not work on this day. They also do not drive, spend money, talk on the phone, or turn on electricity. Instead, they go to synagogue, take long walks, visit friends, and discuss the section of the Torah that was read during morning services. Life in Israel can be fairly quiet on *Shabbat*, especially in Orthodox neighborhoods where stores are closed and buses do not run.

(top) On Fridays, the Muslim day of rest, a **muezzin** *summons Muslims to worship at the mosque with a call to prayer.*

(left) This father is helping his daughter bake a braided challah.

Clothes for play and prayer

People wear many different types of clothing in Israel. Most dress in modern-day clothing such as jeans, T-shirts, shorts, running shoes, skirts, and business suits. Others wear the traditional clothing of their **ethnic** group or culture.

Clothes for praying

When religious Jewish men pray, they drape a *tallit*, or prayer shawl, around their shoulders. They also put on *tephillin* for the morning prayers. Each of these boxes has long black leather straps. One box is tied to the forehead, the other to the left arm facing the heart. *Tephillin* symbolize that a person's mind, heart, and body are to be used for good and not for evil. Religious men always wear a *kippa*, or skullcap, on their head as a sign of modesty before God. Men who are less religious might only wear a *kippa* when they are praying or when they are at a Jewish celebration.

(right) A Jewish boy wears the clothing of prayer. Inside the small black boxes of the **tephillin** *is a prayer: "Hear, oh, Israel. The Lord our God. The Lord is one."*

Chassidic Jews

Chassidic (pronounced ha-si-dic) means "pious ones." *Chassidic* Jews are a group of **ultra-Orthodox Jews** who reject many modern ways. They believe strongly in modesty. When women marry, they shave their heads or keep their hair covered with a wig or scarf. The men have full beards, very short hair, and *peyot*, or side curls. They wear wide-brimmed black hats, long black coats, white shirts, and a *tallit katan*, or small prayer shawl. **Chassidic** *men often wear special fur hats on* **Shabbat.**

Muslim Arabs

Many Muslims follow strict religious rules when choosing what to wear. They dress simply and modestly, according to the Qur'an's instructions. Very **devout** women and girls must cover their bodies completely in public. Men and boys must cover themselves from the waist to the knees. Many men observe these rules by wearing loose fitting pants and shirts. Others wear more traditional clothing. Religious women might wear a long black gown over their clothes, a scarf to cover their head, a veil to cover their face, and gloves to cover their hands. Religious men might wear a robe that comes down to their ankles or loose pants with a long shirt on top. This long, loose clothing protects them from the sun and keeps them cool in the hot weather.

(above) One Arab man dresses in modern clothing while another wears traditional dress, including a **kaffiyeh.** *The kaffiyeh is folded in half diagonally, draped over the head, and held in place with a double ring of black rope, called an* **akkal.**

(above) On special occasions Bedouin women wear elaborate costumes. Veils decorated with coins cover these women's faces.

(left) A young Muslim boy yanks at his mother's head scarf to attract her attention.

23

Art

Art in Israel is as varied as the people who live in the country. Each group of people has its own artistic specialty, whether it is making intricate jewelry, building elaborate mosques, or weaving rich tapestries. Yet the groups also learn from each other and influence one another's work.

Jewish art

Jewish art in Israel is a mixture of styles and themes. Paintings and sculptures have traditionally been based on stories from the Torah, events in history, and people's love of the country. One subject that is often portrayed in Jewish art is the Holocaust, when six million European Jews were killed by the Nazis.

For the first part of the twentieth century, artists in Israel were influenced by the style of the Bezalel Academy of Arts and Crafts. The Bezalel was founded in Jerusalem in 1906. Its goal was to create an original Jewish style of art that combined techniques from Europe and the Middle East. More recently, artists have begun to experiment with different techniques and are exploring themes, such as nature, relationships, and emotions, that have meaning to people wherever they live.

(above) This Jewish bride, originally from the Arab country of Yemen, wears a heavy headdress for her wedding.

(top) Children tumble on Dan Caravan's sculpture, White City, in Tel Aviv.

Muslim art

Muslim art is full of intricate patterns and designs that wind together flowers, vines, stars, and interesting geometric shapes and lines. These designs, called arabesques, can be seen in elaborate mosaics, finely carved wooden doors, and richly colored rugs. Some of the best examples of Islamic art are found on Muslim buildings, especially mosques.

Muslims believe that only Allah can create living things. Showing humans and animals in art, especially in the art of religious buildings, is discouraged. The Dome of the Rock, in Jerusalem, is considered the first Muslim masterpiece of art. It has no pictures of animals or people, and was designed to honor the Muslim faith.

(below) Intricate tiles and Arabic calligraphy decorate the Dome of the Rock.

Calligraphy

Muslims believe the Qur'an to be Allah's exact words, so they spend a lot of time making this holy book look beautiful. They use calligraphy, or fine writing, and decorate the Qur'an with arabesques. Quotations from the Qur'an and Muhammad's sayings, written in calligraphy, also decorate buildings, tiles, pottery, wood, and metalware.

It takes a steady hand to paint ceramic tiles in the elaborate Armenian style.

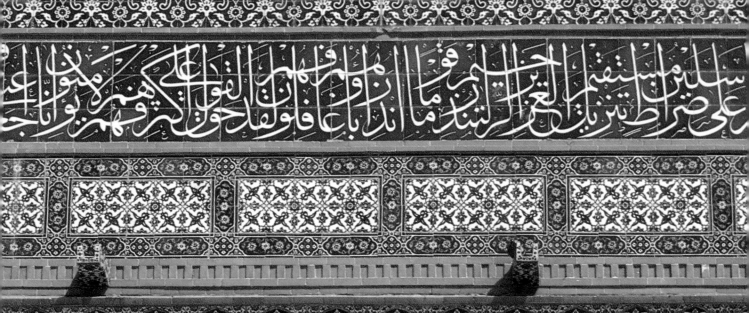

Whether listening to the radio, singing around the campfire, or chanting prayers, music is an important part of life in Israel. Some music has its roots in the Bible or Qur'an. Other music has more modern themes that are not based on religion. Hebrew folk songs, for example, express people's hope for permanent peace in a country that has fought many wars.

In Israel's main cities there are concerts and events almost every night. You might have your choice between going to see the Israel Philharmonic Orchestra, a band from North America or Europe, or an Israeli singer who plays traditional Middle Eastern instruments. There is something for almost everyone.

Middle Eastern instruments

Imagine playing the same kind of instrument that people played over a thousand years ago! Here are some Middle Eastern instruments that have their origins in ancient **civilizations**.

*The **tabla** is a hand drum shaped like a vase. Traditional **tablas** have goat skin, or even fish skin, stretched over the top.*

*The **qanun** has 81 strings. To play the **qanun**, you pluck the strings with your forefingers.*

*The **nai** is a very basic flute. There are six holes for the fingers, a hole for the thumb, and a hole to blow across.*

*The **oud** is similar to the lute. Its strings are plucked, sometimes with a trimmed eagle's feather.*

Daff *is the Arabic word for tambourine. The metal disks jingle when it is shaken.*

*The **mizmar** has a double reed. Its sound is powerful, similar to that of bagpipes!*

Can I have this dance?

In Israel, ever since ancient times, dance has been a way to express joy. Foot-stomping, hand-clapping folk dances are a large part of many celebrations.

The debka

Whether you are celebrating a baby's birth, a wedding, or the end of the harvest, dancing the *debka* may be part of the festivities. This Arab folk dance has many different steps. Some are performed only by men, some only by women, and others by both. You can dance the *debka* in a circle or in a line, changing the formation in the middle of the song.

Dance the hora

The most famous Jewish folk dance is the *hora*. The *hora* was first danced in Romania, but now it is danced at Jewish celebrations around the world. Try the *hora* in a circle or in a line as you and your friends wind your way around the room. Here's what to do:

❶ Step to the right with your right foot.
❷ Cross your left foot behind the right.
❸ Step to the right with your right foot.
❹ Hop on your right foot and swing your left foot across the front of your right foot.
❺ Step in place with your left foot.
❻ Hop on your left foot and swing your right foot across the front of your left foot.
❼ Repeat until the song is over.

A crowd claps out the rhythm for a dancer at a Moroccan Jewish celebration.

How do you say ...?

Hebrew and Arabic are Israel's official languages, but you can hear a variety of other languages on the street. In fact, many people in Israel speak three languages, including English.

Hebrew

Over 2000 years ago, Hebrew was the language of the Jewish people. It was the language of the Torah and the language that people spoke every day. Through time, as Jews scattered to different countries, Hebrew as a spoken language died out. It remained a written language of religious study.

In the late nineteenth century, Eliezer Ben-Yehuda created a new spoken language from the ancient written language of the Torah. He had **immigrated** to Palestine, as Israel was then called, from Eastern Europe and decided that Jewish people coming to the country from around the world needed a common language. He convinced settlers to speak Hebrew and began to record the new language in a dictionary. When Eliezer Ben-Yehuda started

speaking Hebrew, there were only 7500 words. Now there are more than 100,000!

Yiddish

Yiddish is a language spoken mostly by older Jews from Eastern Europe. It is a mixture of medieval German and Hebrew. Many ultra-Orthodox Jews speak Yiddish. They believe that Hebrew is a holy language and should only be used for prayer.

Arabic

Arabic is spoken by about 15 percent of Israel's population. Most of these people are Arabs, some are Druze, and some are Jews from Middle Eastern and African countries. There are two types of Arabic: one is used in everyday conversation and one is used in writing or in more formal situations, such as radio and television news broadcasts, plays, and movies. The Qur'an is written in formal Arabic. Even if a Muslim's first language is not Arabic, he or she still prays in this language.

This food stand sells more than just fruit juice. Do you recognize any of the signs?

Practice your Hebrew and Arabic

Hebrew and Arabic each have their own alphabet. Hebrew has 22 letters. Five of these letters look different when they are at the end of a word. Vowels are shown using dots and dashes. Arabic has 28 letters and uses a dot system to show vowel sounds.

A beginner's dictionary

English	Hebrew		Arabic	
Hello	Shalom	שלום	Marhaba	مرحباً
Good morning	Boker tov	בוקר טוב	Sabah el khier	صباح الخير
Good evening	Erev tov	ארב טוב	Misa el khier	مساء الخير
Good night	Layla tov	לילה טוב	Tesbah ala khier	تصبح على خير
Goodbye	Shalom	שלום	Ma-ah-salameh	مع السلامة
Yes	Ken	כן	Na'am	نعم
No	Lo	לא	La	لا
Excuse me	Slichah	סליחה	Ismach lee	إسمح لي
Please	Bevakashah	בבקשה	Min fadlak	من فضلك
Thank you	Todah	תודה	Shoukran	شكراً

(left) Customers browse through piles of books during the annual Hebrew Book Week.

Hebrew and Arabic are written from right to left. That is the opposite direction to how English is written. The front cover of the Hebrew picture book that this boy is reading would be the back cover of an English book.

29

In print and on the air

People in Israel love to read newspapers, especially the big weekend papers that are published on Fridays. They also enjoy watching the news on television and listening to hourly news broadcasts on the radio. This news-gathering habit started many years ago when Israel was at war with its neighbors and the people of the country needed to know if they were in danger. Israel is not at war today, but like people everywhere Israelis still want to know what is happening in their country and around the world.

Two Arabs pour over the latest news as their friend passes on the headlines to people passing by.

Satellite dishes jostle for space on the already crowded rooftops of Old Jerusalem.

On the radio

There is a lot more on the radio beside the news. You can listen to music, talk shows, traffic reports, and special children's programs in many different languages. There is even one station for people who have come to Israel from other countries. For example, immigrants from the former Soviet Union can listen to programs in Russian and people from Ethiopia can listen to programs in their language, Amharic.

The TV guide

Until a few years ago, Israel had just one television channel and it was on the air for only seven hours a day. If your television had an antenna and you pointed the antenna in just the right direction, you might have been able to tune in to programs from neighboring countries such as Egypt, Jordan, Cyprus, or Lebanon. In 1993, Israel's second channel began broadcasting. Cable television came to most of the country a year later. Today, if you have cable, you can receive over 40 channels and watch programs from countries such as the United States, France, Germany, India, Italy, Morocco, Spain, Russia, and Turkey. Children in Israel are learning words from many different languages just by watching TV!

Tell me a story

Storytelling is an age-old tradition. In Israel, as in other countries around the world, people tell tales of wonder and amazement, tales from history and from their holy books. Here is a traditional story that you can tell others.

Raffi the tailor had a large family and a very small house. His seven children were crowded into one bed. Raffi and his wife, Rachel, slept on the kitchen floor below the dripping clothesline.

One day, just before Pesach, Raffi brought down the holiday dishes from the eaves. Now the kitchen was even more crowded. "Raffi!" Rachel cried, "This house is too small to have a Pesach seder. DO something!!"

Raffi hurried to the rabbi. "What am I to do?" he cried. "My wife says our house is too small for a seder." The rabbi looked wisely at Raffi. "Bring your three goats into the house."

Raffi pulled the stubborn goats into the house. They clattered about, clamored onto the bed, and pulled at the dangling laundry in the kitchen.

Raffi hurried to the rabbi. "Help! The house is even smaller. What should I do now?" "Bring in your rooster, your ten chickens, and your four geese," the rabbi ordered.

"Koo-kooroo-koo-koooo!" the rooster announced from the clothesline as the goats banged around in confusion. Chickens flew about in a gust of feathers, and the geese waddled round and round the kitchen table.

"*Oy vey*!" Raffi stuffed his fingers into his ears and ran full-tilt to the rabbi. "The house is smaller than ever," he moaned. "What should I do NOW?" "Now," said the rabbi gravely, "take the goats, the chickens, the geese, and the rooster, and put them outside."

"Get out, shoo, shoo!" Raffi, Rachel, and the children clapped their hands and waved their arms about. Out the door and back to their barnyard the animals went. Raffi, Rachel, and the children slammed the door and leaned huffing and puffing against the doorway. They surveyed the scene in front of them.

"Our rabbi, he is a true miracle worker," cried Rachel in amazement. "Our little house is huge! Now we can invite all of our friends to the seder!"

31

Glossary

atonement The act of asking for forgiveness for sins

Bedouin Arabic tribes who move from place to place in the desert in search of grazing land and water for their livestock

civilization A society with a well-established culture that has existed for a long period of time

crucify To put to death by nailing to a cross

culture The customs, beliefs, and arts of a distinct group of people

devout Devoted to religion

ethnic Describing or relating to social groups connected by race, language, heritage, or religion

faith Religious beliefs

harvest The gathering of crops

holy Having special religious importance

immigrate To come to settle in a different country

monk A member of a male religious community who has taken certain vows, such as silence or poverty

pilgrimage A religious journey to a sacred place

prophet A person who is believed to speak on behalf of God

rabbi A Jewish religious leader

sacrifice To offer to a god

scribe A person who copies manuscripts and documents

self-discipline The ability to control one's feelings and actions

spiritual center A holy gathering place for people of the same religion

traditional Describing customs that are handed down from one generation to another

ultra-Orthodox Jew A Jewish person who closely follows the religion's ancient laws and traditions

Index

1 2 3 4 5 6 7 8 9 0 Printed in the USA 5 4 3 2 1 0 9 8